SIDEKICK

the video games mental health journal

in aid of

Published by Peregrine Coast Press
peregrinecoast.press
@press_peregrine

ISBN 978-1-915826-04-6

First Printing, May 2023.

Printed and bound by Standart Impressa
Stock: 100gsm MultiOffset
Covers: 250gsm matte-laminated Alaska Arktika
Typefaces: Ingra, Chalkboard, Palmer Lake

Please note this work is unaffiliated with Thunder Lotus Games, Ninja Theory, Bennett Foddy, Naughty Dog, Glumberland, Infinite Fall, Secret Lab, Mike Bithell, or Toby Fox.

Our mission at Safe In Our World is simple. We are creating and fostering worldwide mental health awareness within the video game industry to eliminate the stigma surrounding mental health, make it a natural topic of discussion, and to promote dialogue around mental health so people are not afraid to reach out for help if they need it.

This journal is a huge part of that mission. Normalising talking about how we feel and identifying our emotions is crucial for taking care of ourselves. Which is why we've created this book: to help you keep track and reflect on your wellbeing. Of course, it wouldn't be Safe In Our World without video games, so we're sure you'll recognise a few references in here...

If you need help, visit our website
safeinourworld.org

Peregrine Coast Press is a publishing co-operative based in the UK and US. Like other co-operatives, we operate with a flat hierarchy and every worker-member owns an equal share of the company.

We specialise in books, games, and books about games.

You can find out more about our work at
peregrinecoast.press

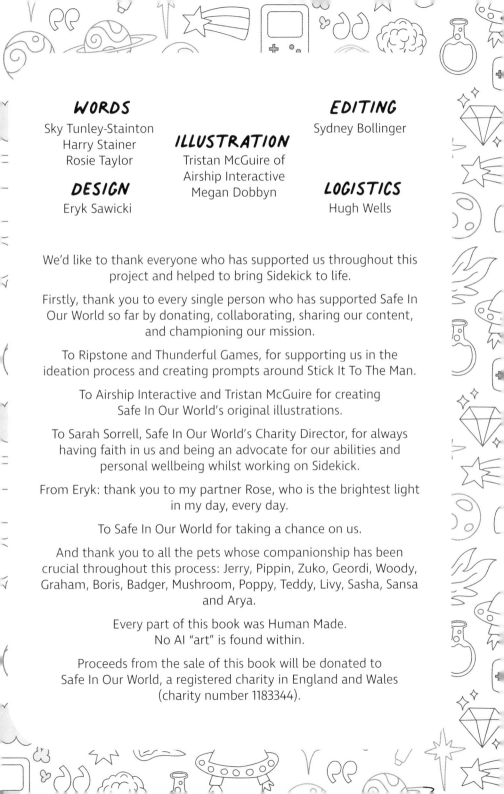

WORDS

Sky Tunley-Stainton
Harry Stainer
Rosie Taylor

ILLUSTRATION

Tristan McGuire of
Airship Interactive
Megan Dobbyn

DESIGN

Eryk Sawicki

EDITING

Sydney Bollinger

LOGISTICS

Hugh Wells

We'd like to thank everyone who has supported us throughout this project and helped to bring Sidekick to life.

Firstly, thank you to every single person who has supported Safe In Our World so far by donating, collaborating, sharing our content, and championing our mission.

To Ripstone and Thunderful Games, for supporting us in the ideation process and creating prompts around Stick It To The Man.

To Airship Interactive and Tristan McGuire for creating Safe In Our World's original illustrations.

To Sarah Sorrell, Safe In Our World's Charity Director, for always having faith in us and being an advocate for our abilities and personal wellbeing whilst working on Sidekick.

From Eryk: thank you to my partner Rose, who is the brightest light in my day, every day.

To Safe In Our World for taking a chance on us.

And thank you to all the pets whose companionship has been crucial throughout this process: Jerry, Pippin, Zuko, Geordi, Woody, Graham, Boris, Badger, Mushroom, Poppy, Teddy, Livy, Sasha, Sansa and Arya.

Every part of this book was Human Made.
No AI "art" is found within.

I could see that in people. See the cracks in them. It's easy, light shines through.

—SPIRITFARER, THUNDER LOTUS GAMES (2020)

THIS JOURNAL BELONGS TO:

SIDEKICK

Use this space to empty your brain, if you need to.

STRESS

If you've ever played Dark Souls, you've likely experienced what stress is. Stress causes physical changes in the body designed to help you take on threats or difficulties.

You might notice that your heart pounds, your breathing quickens, your muscles tense, and you start to sweat – this is often called the "fight or flight" response. Once the threat or difficulty passes, these physical effects usually fade.

But if you're constantly stressed, your body stays in a state of high alert and you could develop stress-related symptoms.

Stress is something that's difficult to define or measure. Some people thrive on a busy lifestyle and are able to cope well with daily stresses. However, some people find that even a tiny change from their normal routine can cause stress. Most people fall somewhere in between but may experience periods in which stress levels increase.

Overleaf you'll find some tips for dealing with stress.

POSITIVE RELAXATION

Set specific times aside to relax positively.

Don't just let relaxation happen, or not happen, at the mercy of work, family, etc. Plan it and look forward to it. Different people prefer different things.

A long bath, a quiet stroll, sitting and just playing your favourite game, etc. These times are not wasteful and you should not feel guilty about not 'getting on with things'. They can be times of reflection and putting life back in perspective.

MOVEMENT

Many people feel that regular movement reduces their level of stress. Any exercise is good, but try to plan for at least 30 minutes of movement at least five days a week. A brisk walk on most days is a good start if you are not used to exercise.

HOBBIES

Many people find that a hobby which has no deadlines or pressures and which can be picked up or left easily, takes the mind off stresses. Such hobbies include, for example: sports, knitting, music, model-making, puzzles and reading for pleasure.

TIME OUT

Try to allow several times a day to 'stop' and take some time out. For example, getting up 15-20 minutes earlier than you need to is a good start. You can use this time to think about and plan the coming day and to prepare for the day's events unrushed. Take a regular and proper lunch break, preferably away from work. Don't work over lunch. Even if work is busy, try to take 5-10 minutes away every few hours to relax.

Once or twice a week, try to plan some time just to be alone and unobtainable. For example, a gentle stroll or a sit in the park often helps to break out of life's hustle and bustle.

Try a bit of colouring to relax and alleviate stress.

THE HARDEST BATTLES
ARE FOUGHT IN THE MIND,
NOT WITH THE SWORD.
—HELLBLADE: SENUA'S SACRIFICE,
NINJA THEORY (2017)

Imagine all of your stress in a bucket. As more stress pours in, the bucket gets heavier and harder to carry. You need to find ways to empty the bucket and lighten the load.

Use the image below to visualise your stress and how you cope. In the rain clouds, write some things that are causing you stress. Then, label the taps at the bottom with some of the activities that help you cope. As these taps are turned on, your stress should reduce and drain out of the bucket.

Think about whether all of your taps are working.
Do you need to ask someone to help you fix them?

SIDEKICK

Top 3 things about this week

_____

_____

_____

Why are you proud of yourself today?

_____

_____

_____

_____

_____

Why are your loved ones proud of you? (Yes, go and ask them!)

_____

_____

_____

_____

_____

Sometimes it's hard to remember the things that make you amazing. It's okay to lean on others until you believe it yourself.

What are your goals for tomorrow?

_____

_____

_____

_____

_____

We all have moments in life when things can get a bit overwhelming. Let's make sure you have the tools to bring yourself back to reality when things get to be too much.

DEEP BREATHING EXERCISE

If you do this a few times and concentrate fully on breathing, you may find it quite relaxing. Some people find that moving from chest breathing to tummy (abdominal) breathing can be helpful.

Sitting quietly, try putting one hand on your chest and the other on your tummy.

You should aim to breathe quietly by moving your tummy, with your chest moving very little.

This encourages the diaphragm to work efficiently and may help you avoid over-breathing.

MUSCULAR TENSING AND STRETCHING

Try twisting your neck around each way as far as it is comfortable and then relax. Try fully tensing your shoulder and back muscles for several seconds and then relax completely.

SENSORY STIMULATION

Sometimes in moments where you're struggling to focus, it can help to use external stimuli to deliberately shift your focus.

Some people have self-support packs, which include stress balls, puzzles, strong-tasting foods, and/or strong smelling items to help ground them.

What would you have in your self-support pack?

When using sensory items, ask yourself:

- What does it feel like?
- What does it taste like?
- What temperature is it?
- How does this fit together?

It's important to explore the relationship between your mood and your food. Note down a favourite recipe - perhaps it holds nostalgia, or comfort, or joy...

Ingredients

_____
_____
_____
_____
_____
_____
_____

NAME
_____

SERVES

① ② ④ ⑥ ⑧

TIME TO PREPARE
_____

TIME TO COOK
_____

Recipe

_____
_____
_____
_____
_____
_____
_____
_____
_____
_____
_____
_____
_____

We're introduced to thousands of characters through the games we play, and these characters can often serve as role models with ideas and actions just as worthy of admiration as any real person. Use this space to think about videogame characters you admire, and why...

SIDEKICK

Roguelikes have become a staple of modern gaming: games like Hades, Slay the Spire, and Darkest Dungeon all have an incredibly challenging-but-satisfying gameplay loop. Sometimes, your run will go on for hours, and other times you'll only make it through a few rooms, but either way you are compelled to try again.

Our mental wellbeing is the same: we have good days where we feel we can take on the world, and days where even getting out of bed is an immense challenge. Roguelikes have taught us that being overwhelmed is not a failure - it's just part of the process. Similarly, our journey with mental health is not always about winning, but trying again and again, slowly learning how to get better.

1 Start your adventure here.

What can you bring with you to help you on your journey?

2 You've encountered a problem. For example: a difficult task at work or school.

What can you do to solve the problem?

3 You're struggling a little and need to heal.

What self-care activity can you do during the day to feel better?

4 You're almost there!

What else can help you achieve your goals today?

5 Congratulations! You made it through the day.

Now choose your reward: how will you wind down, or what can you do to recognise your achievement?

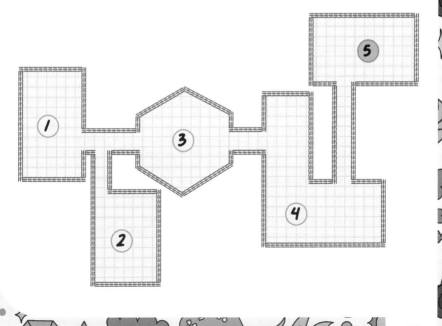

SIDEKICK

This page is reserved for your work meeting doodles, phone call doodles, anxious doodles... anything you want to draw, you can do it here. Go wild.

What does your perfect self-care day look like? Fill in this schedule to design a day that you know is going to look after your mental health. Whenever you need it, come back to this spread and remind yourself of the things you can do to make yourself feel better!

TIME	ACTIVITY

SIDEKICK

Sometimes battling mental health can feel like a really tough boss battle. Use the space below to visualise your anxiety, depression, stress, or other condition as a videogame boss.

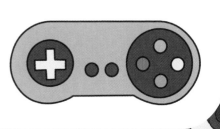

Remember, all bosses can be defeated! What are your boss's weaknesses and what can you do to actively stop this boss from overcoming you? For some, taking medication might help defeat this boss, but for others it might be meditation. Note down what you need to help you win this fight...

Many of us have been playing games for as long as we can remember. Take some time to reflect on the games you loved growing up.

_____
_____
_____
_____
_____
_____
_____
_____
_____
_____
_____
_____
_____
_____
_____
_____
_____
_____
_____
_____

Oh no, it happened *again*.
Oh no, it happened *again*.
Oh no, it happened *again*.
Oh no, it happened *again*.
Oh no, it happened *again*.

Keep on trying,
don't let it get to you.

—Getting Over It
with *Bennett Foddy*
Bennett Foddy (2017)

Every now and then we all need a care package. They can be an important part of maintaining wellbeing and reminding yourself that you are loved and worthy of self-care. Using the prompts below, design your perfect gaming self-care package.

What games are included?

What snacks and drinks would be in there?

What cosy or comforting items would you like?

Sometimes it can be hard to just draw something. If you need a little help with ideas, try to form these shapes into something new...

Create a playlist of your favourite music from video games. Maybe it's something you'll listen to while working or studying, or something you'd bring with you on a long journey. Think about how this music makes you feel.

1. _____

2. _____

3. _____

4. _____

5. _____

6. _____

7. _____

8. _____

9. _____

10. _____

11. _____

12. _____

13. _____

14. _____

15. _____

16. _____

17. _____

18. _____

19. _____

20. _____

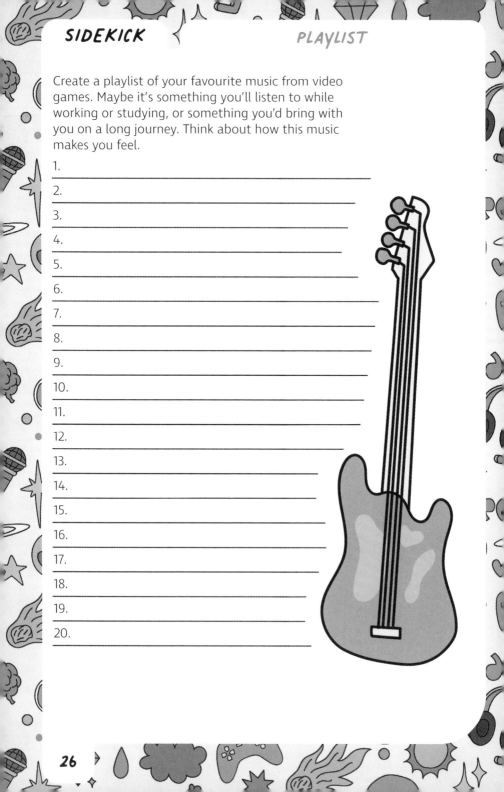

Bottling stuff up inside can have a negative effect on your mental wellbeing, so we present to you... a worry page!

If you're comfortable, use this space to write down any fears, worries or thoughts you feel you want to get out of your head. Hopefully putting them out in the world can offer you some perspective and relieve the pressure of some of these thoughts.

SIDEKICK

Beloved characters like Senua or Madeline may venture on their journeys while not feeling their best: in fact, sometimes it can be a struggle to even get out of bed. 5 in 100 adults experience depression each year. Anyone can develop it, and there isn't an exact known cause. Some people may experience bouts of depression, however others will live with depression for much longer periods of time.

Many people try to cope with depression without realising they are unwell. It's important to get to know yourself and the signs that you might be depressed, or nearing a depressive episode.

Use this space to list some of your personal warning signs of depression or mental ill health:

_____

_____

_____

_____

_____

_____

_____

_____

While depression may require support from a doctor or mental health practitioner, there are things that can be done to mitigate symptoms of depression, either by yourself or with the support of friends and loved ones. It may be useful to share this information with others around you, so they can support you in spotting the signs and connecting you with tools that can help.

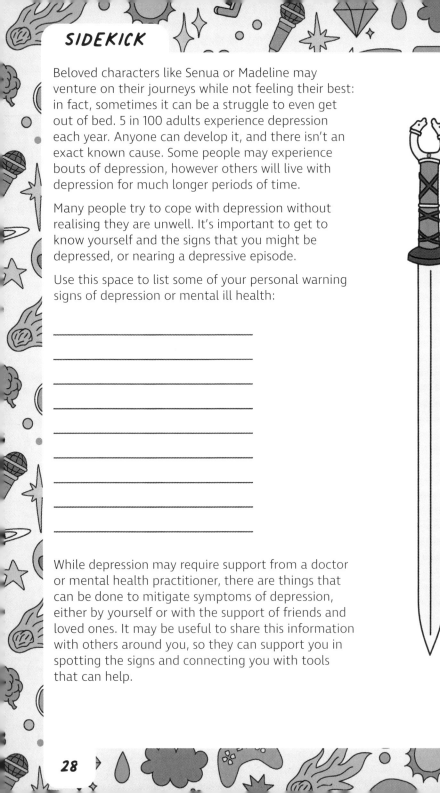

he Last of Us Part I Naughty Dog (2013)

struggled for a long time with
urviving. And no matter what, you
eep finding something to fight for.

Your achievements are worth celebrating!

Did you finally beat Malenia in Elden Ring? Or maybe you overcame your fear and gave a presentation?

Write 5 of your achievements here - big or small - and remember why you're proud of yourself.

I achieved: _____

I'm proud of this because: _____

I achieved: _____

I'm proud of this because: _____

I achieved: _____

I'm proud of this because: _____

I achieved: _____

I'm proud of this because: _____

I achieved: _____

I'm proud of this because: _____

Now let's look forward! Whatever your goals are for the coming year, list them below as motivation to achieve.

_____
_____
_____
_____
_____
_____
_____
_____
_____
_____
_____
_____
_____
_____
_____
_____
_____
_____
_____

SIDEKICK

What do these emotions look like to you? Draw or colour in the spaces below.

HAPPINESS

SADNESS

ANXIETY

DEPRESSION

ANGER

LOVE

STICK IT TO THE MAN!

Ray, the hero in '**Stick It To The Man**', discovers that they can use the power of their brain to transform the world around them.

With practice, they learn that they can tear, sticker and craft solutions to any challenges they face.

We know it's not as easy IRL, but filling this journal is a fantastic way to organise your thoughts and emotions, gain control of your thinking and shape your own winning reality.

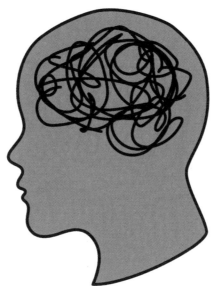

This exercise can help you quickly shift awareness to your breath and the present moment. Before starting, find a quiet space with a comfortable chair.

Place the tip of your pencil on the blue starting dot • and bring your attention to your breath.

What sensations do you notice? Can you feel the air in your nose? Does your chest rise?

Now, slowly move your pencil along the blue dotted line, breathing in gently as you go. When you reach the first pink dotted line, continue at the same pace but breathe out. Repeat the process, breathing in on the blue dotted lines and out on the pink dotted lines.

No two lines are the same shape or length; notice how this subtly changes each breath you take. If your attention wanders, simply return your awareness back to the page and your breath.

How do you feel after this exercise? Many people find that focusing all of their attention on something simple helps them to relax and destress.

It's important to explore the relationship between your mood and your food. Note down a favourite recipe - perhaps it holds nostalgia, or comfort, or joy...

Ingredients

_____
_____
_____
_____
_____
_____
_____

Recipe

NAME
_____

SERVES
◇1 ◇2 ◇4 ◇6 ◇8

TIME TO PREPARE
_____

TIME TO COOK
_____

_____
_____
_____
_____
_____
_____
_____
_____
_____
_____
_____
_____
_____

God of War Ragnarök shows us the power of poetry through the snippets Kratos finds on his journey. Creative writing is a great way to focus your mind: using the space below, try to write a poem. It doesn't have to rhyme and don't worry about whether it's good — just give it a go.

When you look in the mirror,
what do you see?

Have you ever explored a videogame world and thought 'I could live here'?

Let's take a closer look at that feeling: what video game worlds make you feel calm and why? It could be as simple as your cosy Animal Crossing village, or a place that's tied to nostalgia. Feel free to write, doodle, and create a reminder of a gaming world that makes you feel at home.

If you've played games like Stardew Valley, Animal Crossing, My Time at Portia, or Ooblets (to name a few), you'll be familiar with the relaxing, cosy atmosphere of the farming sim. One of the primary themes of these games is getting to know the villagers by building relationships with them and receiving support from them.

True to life, the closer you get with these villagers, the more they open up and allow you to learn about them. As you forge stronger relationships, they will begin to offer you advice and support as you continue on your journey through the game. Sometimes they'll give you gifts, or simply say something to brighten your day. What we can learn from this is the importance of valuing your relationships and supporting your friends.

You probably have some real-life friends who have helped you along your journey, too. Try writing a letter to a friend who has helped you through a difficult time. How did they help? How can you thank them?

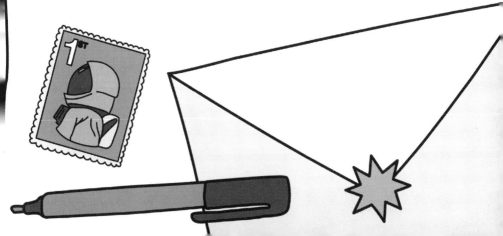

SIDEKICK

Having an emotional response to a videogame can be a big part of what makes them mean a lot to us. This could be anything from the heart-wrenching opening to The Last of Us or the side-splitting comedy of Portal 2.

List out some moments in games that made you laugh, cry, or emotionally moved you in a way you haven't forgotten.

This page is reserved for your work meeting doodles, phone call doodles, anxious doodles... anything you want to draw, you can do it here. Go wild.

SIDEKICK

You're about to set off on an adventure...
Games let you create characters all the time
so why don't you use the space below to draw
your own. Get creative and give them a name
and write what type of game they are going
to be in. Is it a fun adventure? Or maybe a
post-apocalyptic journey across a wasteland?
It's completely up to you.

OOBLETS

I recently learned that I can like things even if everyone else likes those same things.

—GLUMBERLAND (2020)

Burnout can take many forms, but is chiefly characterised by a state of physical and emotional exhaustion caused by long-term stress, and a physically or emotionally demanding environment.

It can be difficult to identify burnout until the physical effects of it become severe, but you might be able to recognise feeling:

- constantly tired or drained
- hopeless
- detached
- overwhelmed

Whether it's work, school, your social life, or even gaming, it's important to find balance and understand when you might be taking on too much. Use the space below to list some of your personal warning signs of approaching burnout.

_____

_____

_____

_____

_____

_____

_____

_____

_____

_____

Whatever you want to say to your past self,
you can say it here.

SIDEKICK

Connecting with others can be crucial when it comes to looking after your wellbeing, and luckily games can bring us together in a variety of meaningful ways. Take some time to think about when games have brought you closer to others: maybe online, split-screen, or just spending time with those you care about.

Often characters in games have to step outside of their comfort zone in order to grow, be it Aloy choosing to journey into the Forbidden West, or Beatrix LeBeau, the Slime Rancher moving away to a far off planet. Exploring something new, or unknown, can be incredibly scary but equally rewarding.

Write about a time you have stepped outside of your comfort zone: how did it feel? What about that situation made you proud?

MY GAMES BACKLOG

We both know you'll probably play that one game four more times this year instead of looking at your backlog, but hey, it's nice to write them down and hope, right?

Top 3 things about this week

_____
_____
_____

Why are you proud of yourself today?

_____
_____
_____
_____
_____

Why are your loved ones proud of you? (Yes, go and ask them!)

_____
_____
_____
_____
_____

Sometimes it's hard to remember the things that make you amazing. It's okay to lean on others until you believe it yourself.

What are your goals for tomorrow?

_____
_____
_____
_____
_____

Emotional literacy is the process of better understanding the emotions you feel: it can help you to recognise when these feelings arise, as well as to express them in a healthy manner. "Emotional labelling" is a phrase used to describe the act of naming your emotions with greater specificity, which can lead to increased understanding and emotional literacy.

Some examples of deeper emotional labelling could include the following:

Sad	Happy	Angry	Anxious
Disappointed	Thankful	Frustrated	Stressed
Regretful	Content	Annoyed	Afraid
Paralysed	Excited	Defensive	Vulnerable
Mournful	Confident	Disgusted	Confused
Disillusioned	Relaxed	Spiteful	Worried

How are you feeling now?

_____

SIDEKICK

One of the key aspects of video games that makes them so powerful is the ability to walk in other people's shoes - no other medium offers us this unique perspective. Games give us an insight into the experiences of people with different genders, abilities, races, societal classes, and more.

Games like Before I Forget, Life Is Strange, and Another Day allow us to understand worldviews & circumstances that are special and can be different from our own. Taking the power of video-game storytelling and applying it to our own wellbeing allows us to treat others with kindness and empathy - there is great meaning in understanding each other despite our differences and in doing so we can look after one another including all of our mental health.

Think about a time when you have played as a character who is different from yourself. What did you learn about their worldview? Did they teach you more about a specific subject? Or maybe you learned to understand a certain community? Use the space below to explore how a game allowed you to open your mind more and understand the world a little better.

It's important to explore the relationship between your mood and your food. Note down a favourite recipe - perhaps it holds nostalgia, or comfort, or joy...

Ingredients

_____
_____
_____
_____
_____
_____
_____

NAME

_____

SERVES

◇ 1   ◇ 2   ◇ 4   ◇ 6   ◇ 8

TIME TO PREPARE

_____

TIME TO COOK

_____

Recipe

_____
_____
_____
_____
_____
_____
_____
_____
_____
_____
_____
_____

As we know by now, games can speak volumes; the storytelling and dialogue can be just as powerful as film and TV. Think of some of your favourite quotes from video games - the ones that really left their mark - and write them below.

Thomas had a new theory. The world was training him. He could feel himself getting smarter.

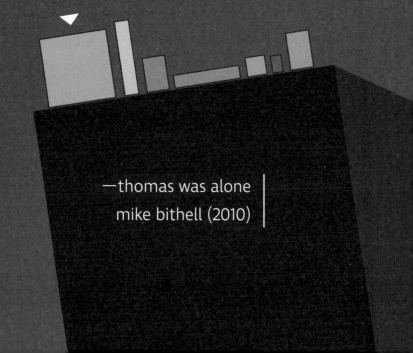

—thomas was alone
mike bithell (2010)

Within this book you have learned ways to manage your wellbeing, express your feelings, and share your love of games. Now, it's all you! Use the rest of this book to write, draw, doodle, list, and everything in between!

SIDEKICK

SIDEKICK

SIDEKICK

SIDEKICK

SIDEKICK

SIDEKICK

SIDEKICK

SIDEKICK

SIDEKICK

SIDEKICK

SIDEKICK

SIDEKICK

SIDEKICK

SIDEKICK

SIDEKICK

SIDEKICK

* Despite everything, it's still you. *

-Undertale, Toby Fox (2015)